to Grab Your Life by the Throat and Really Make it Happen!

© ℗ Peter Thomson Leamington Spa 2000

✅ Introduction

Hello…. and welcome to *117 Ways to Achieve **More….** Making it Happen!* Already I know that you are someone who wants to make a positive difference to your life!

With this booklet :

You are going to be more in control of your life, your actions and your results.

You are going to be more creative every single day.

You are going to be wealthier, whatever your definition of wealth.

You will have the right attitude to life and treat everything that happens to you as part of a great adventure.

In short, you will be the best you can be at everything you decide to do. How can I make such bold statements? Simply because the ideas, methods, and thoughts you will read, have been tried and tested and proven throughout history.

Now I don't know how soon you will begin to feel happy about yourself. I don't know how soon you will earn the amount of money you desire. I don't even know how soon you will maximise your potential. What I do know is that those who have already begun the process say to me, 'Peter, these ideas are so simple, so easy to implement, such common sense, that they work all the time!'.

☑ Enthusiastic Action

1. Carpe diem - seize the day! There is a moment in every person's life when the awareness of their destiny bursts like a bubble onto the surface of their conscious mind. This is when the strong will awake and decide to take action to change their world for the better.

2. Take total control of your life. When we take total control we can focus on making a positive difference. Be the one who decides the direction of your life. Make that decision…NOW!

3. Start a company called ME Unlimited! You are to be all the members of the board:

The Chair- Responsible for the attitude which prevails in the company.
The Sales Director- Responsible for the income generation.
The Finance Director- Responsible for the control of the finances, maintaining a budget and accurate records.
The Planning Director- Responsible for goal setting, creating direction and organising dreams into an action plan.
The Human Resources Director- Responsible for health, fitness, diet, and general well-being.
The Mental Resources Director- Responsible for all mental faculties: learning to read faster, soaking up information and other mental resources.
The Research and Development Director- Responsible for understanding and creativity.
The Communications Director- Responsible for communicating effectively, creating rapport with family, friends and colleagues.
The Administration Director- Responsible for all paperwork skills and ensuring that the administration of *Me Unlimited* runs as smoothly as possible.

4 Award each board member a mark out of ten:

The Chair	____
The Sales Director	____
The Finance Director	____
The Planning Director	____
The Human Resources Director	____
The Mental Resources Director	____
The Research and Development Director	____
The Communications Director	____
The Administration Director	____

5 Use your skills and talents to the full. List your talents in the space below. Are you using all these skills to the maximum?

---

6 Make decisions quickly and change your mind slowly. It is often said that this is what successful people do. Too many people jump from job to job, business to business, relationship to relationship. Give things sufficient time to check whether they are right.

7 Change! If you realise you are in the wrong place, having given it your best shot, then change! Imagine it is twenty million years ago. You are asked to bet on whether the dinosaur or the mouse will live longest. I am sure, you like me would have bet on the dinosaur. But the dinosaur was resistant to change!

8 List the reasons for the success you have had. This will give you added perspective on what you need to do for more success.

9 List the reasons for the results you had that you did not want. This will help you avoid doing more of the same!

If you have not yet added your own name to those lists, then I suggest you do. You are the one in control, you are the one responsible, you are the principal player in your life.

10 Accept that 'Everyone is in Sales'. For anyone not directly involved in sales this may be difficult. But you and I know that we are always selling. We persuade drivers to let us in at traffic jams. We hear parents persuading their children to tidy their rooms. We read of union representatives negotiating pay rises.

11 Be persistent. In the race between the tortoise and the hare, who won? The tortoise. Why? Because it was persistent whilst the hare kept dashing off and got bored and gave up!

12 Get a result, there are no failures. The only way that any rough gemstones are made into smooth, highly valuable gemstones is by the application of friction, and that is what life does to us.

13 Read your goals. Do this each day, so that you are focussed on their accomplishment.

14 Be the best you can be. As my wife often says to me, '…who else can you be?'

15 Anticipate things being good. When we do this, they often turn out well or better than they might have done if we were working on the understanding that they would turn out badly.

16 Accept a weakness. Some weaknesses are not holding you back from achieving the major things in your life. So what difference will it make if you change them?

17 Criticise the action, not the person. For example, let's say you attempt to do something and it doesn't work out. Don't go around saying: 'I'm a failure'. Say 'I like myself, I didn't like that particular action and I will not be taking that particular action again'.

18 Fall in love with you again. It is too easy to look for what is missing, or at weaknesses instead of strengths. Next time you are on your own, take off all your clothes. Stand in front of a full-length mirror and fall in love with you again.

19 Learn more. Many people have a number of hours available each day in which to listen to audio tapes. Perhaps while doing work around the house or driving the car. 2 hours a day is 10 hours a week, and 40 hours a month. So much time.

20 Take tests. When we take a test, it is immediately afterwards that our brains are crying out for more information. So it is one of the ways in which we can motivate ourselves to learn more.

Try this test. Write in, or put a ring around a number that represents your feelings in each area. The higher the number the more positive you are about that topic.

I like myself **10** ___ **5** ___ **1** I don't like myself

I'm a winner **10** ___ **5** ___ **1** I'm not a winner

I can learn more **10** ___ **5** ___ **1** There little more to learn

I embrace change **10** ___ **5** ___ **1** I fear change

I'm enthusiastic **10** ___ **5** ___ **1** I'm unenthusiastic

I take 100% responsibility **10** ___ **5** ___ **1** I blame others

I self-talk positively **10** ___ **5** ___ **1** I self-talk negatively

I do hard things first **10** ___ **5** ___ **1** I do hard things last

I'm just the right age **10** ___ **5** ___ **1** I'm too young/old

I learn from rejection **10** ___ **5** ___ **1** I fear rejection

Total score = ___

21 Compare your test results with your last set of results. From this you can see how you have improved. Never compare the results with someone else's. They have different abilities and aims.

☑ Subconscious Encoding

The best garden you will ever have is the garden between your ears. The better the seeds, the better the flowers and the easier they are to harvest. The garden needs tending on a regular basis, so be careful about the seeds you put into the garden between your ears.

22 Be good to the world. This idea is based on the law of cause and effect. Whatever you do (the cause), there will always be a result (the effect). If you smile at the world then the world will reflect that smile back to you.

23 Script your life. Get an A4 pad and a pen, go forward in your mind about five years and then write the story of what's happened to you during the past five years. This is another way of getting into the idea of always having a choice, and being our own leader.

24 Forgive people. Think for a moment about all the people you hate, or may have a grudge against you. Forgive them. If you can get rid of that hate and those grudges, you will be amazed at how much clear space you will create in your mind.

25 Forgive yourself. We all make mistakes in our lives. Don't carry the burden of those mistakes with you, get rid of them.

26 Accept your age. We cannot change our chronological age, we can change our physiological age, by exercise, by diet, by the way in which we live our lives. We can change our attitude about age. 'If you're good enough, you're old enough'. 'If your good enough you're still young enough'.

27 Write positive things about yourself. Use this space:

---

28 Remember the positives. Reaffirm those positives and keep programming them back into the computer that's in your mind. Your subconscious will then keep pushing positive things out. What goes in, must come out.

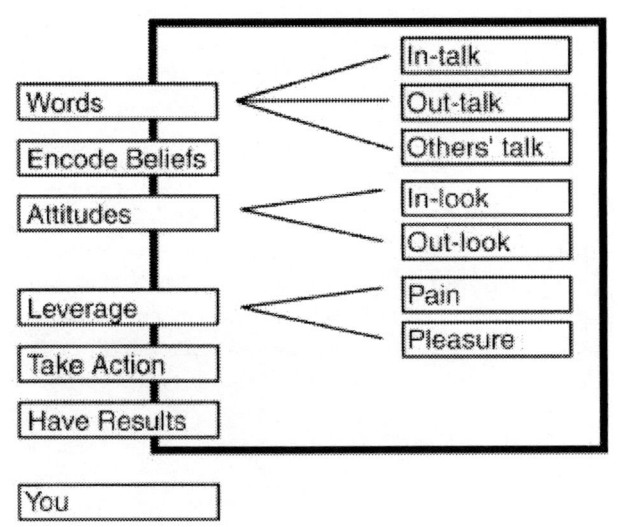

```
┌─────────────────────────────────────────────┐
│                              ┌───────────┐  │
│                          ╱──│ In-talk    │  │
│  ┌──────────┐           ╱    ├───────────┤  │
│  │ Words    │──────────<────│ Out-talk   │  │
│  └──────────┘           ╲    ├───────────┤  │
│  ┌───────────────┐       ╲──│ Others' talk│ │
│  │ Encode Beliefs│          └───────────┘  │
│  └───────────────┘           ┌───────────┐  │
│  ┌──────────┐            ╱──│ In-look    │  │
│  │ Attitudes│────────────<   ├───────────┤  │
│  └──────────┘            ╲──│ Out-look   │  │
│                              └───────────┘  │
│                              ┌───────────┐  │
│  ┌──────────┐            ╱──│ Pain       │  │
│  │ Leverage │────────────<   ├───────────┤  │
│  └──────────┘            ╲──│ Pleasure   │  │
│  ┌──────────────┐            └───────────┘  │
│  │ Take Action  │                           │
│  └──────────────┘                           │
│  ┌──────────────┐                           │
│  │ Have Results │                           │
│  └──────────────┘                           │
└─────────────────────────────────────────────┘
┌──────┐
│ You  │
└──────┘
```

29 Program 'I can' 'I have' 'I do' 'I am' attitudes. 'I am a happy person' 'I do spend time with my children'. It doesn't matter whether you have actually become or done whatever it is you are programming. By telling your mind in *advance* that you have already done something, it will act accordingly. 'What you say will be the way'.

30 Preview review. Before a meeting begins, write a report of what happened. That may sound strange. How can you write a report about what actually took place? Just do it…take a few moments as though you have entered the meeting, had the conversation, completed the meeting and are back at your desk.

31 Play a programming tape. You can easily obtain C10s (just 5 minutes) or C30s (15 minutes). Use these guidelines:

✓ Repeat onto both sides of the tape, your affirmations.
✓ Always use *you* and not I.
✓ There must be no linguistic negatives.
✓ All the statements must be in the present tense.
✓ The In-Talk must be specific.
✓ Ensure there are no side-effects to the programming.
✓ All of these guidelines apply to writing goals as well.

☑ Motivation

Motivation is caused by needs. If we need food, we become motivated, or driven, to find food. We become aware of our surroundings, where we are and if there is food available. There is another strange factor that comes into play in these situations. When we are really hungry, we will eat anything. This is the same with any of the fourteen psychological needs. The fourteen needs are: Pride/Ego, Personal power, Curiosity, Love, Emotional security, Belonging, Recognition of effort, Peer approval, Creativity, Accomplishment, Freedom, Success, Self-esteem, and Winning.

32 Turn psychological needs into drives. Imagine you are at the end of a long room standing by a large block of ice. You are very cold. At the other end of the room is a blazing log fire: that end of the room is warm and comfortable. While you are standing by the ice, you are highly motivated to move away from that pain and towards the pleasure. Set goals that make you aware of the 'away' motivating pain *and* the 'toward' motivating pleasure.

33 Use this three stage process to create drives:

✓ Decide what you want in any situation
✓ Decide what you don't want in any situation
✓ Answer this simple question: 'Why?'

34 Make the pleasure and pain vivid. In your mind's eye, create a box and put all of these motivating factors into that box. Go and sit on one end of a hypothetical see-saw, and have a friend (remember this is only in your mind's eye) carry the box, with difficulty, to one end. It might take a number of people to lift it, for the heavier it is the better. The crowd lifts the box into the air and slams it down onto the end of the see-saw. The result: you shoot up in the air and you are off, you've started to take action. The box was so heavy that you had no choice but to take action.

35 Find a role model. That is to say someone who is already doing what it is you want to do. Then you can ask 'What did they do to accomplish this?' . If you face a particular challenge you can ask 'What would they do in this situation?'

36 Smile. This is one of the great ways to keep on feeling happy, and it is one thing we all know.

37 Focus on opportunities not problems. There was once a shoe manufacturer who sent an experienced salesman to Africa to assess the potential for expansion. He phoned back and said 'I'm coming home, it's a waste of time, no one here wears shoes.' Some years later a young inexperienced salesman was sent out, and he phoned back ' Send three containers of shoes! Its going to be great here…nobody wears shoes!"

38 Think of fear as: False Evidence Appearing Real or Forever Expecting Awful Results or Face it Evalute it Analyse it and Reject it.

39 Recognise mental chains that hold you back. By chains I mean the thoughts that shackle us to ideas we may have of ourselves, or ideas that others may have of us, which are no longer appropriate.

40 Throw away chains that hold you back. Do this by sitting quietly. Think about yourself and what self-limiting beliefs you may have. Then imagine in your mind's eye, ask a friend's opinion. I am sure they will have a different opinion to you. Alternatively, use programming, as discussed earlier.

✓ Rules

Rules and regulations are the boundaries within which we live our lives. 'Whose decision is it when we're offside?' 'Whose decision is it to send us off?' Sometimes, we are just so busy working day to day that we don't take time to find out who set the rules of the game we're playing. It is time we took that time.

41 Agree with the rules that help you. Disagree with the rules that don't help you. I know there have been times in my life I have been glad I disagreed. For example 'Money is the root of all evil' or 'You should get a proper job to fall back on'.

42 Ignore peer group rules. This starts at school, where the 'hard-nuts' don't do their homework or don't hand it in on time. Then at work it becomes 'I always feel bad on Monday mornings, don't you?' and 'Thank god its Friday!'

43 Decide on your own rule for success. If you let magazine ads or TV programmes decide, success becomes hard to achieve. Just as you near the finishing line, someone moves it.

44 Finish this sentence: I am successful when…

45 Try some of these ideas: 'I am successful when… I am alive in the morning, I arrive at work, I am giving it my best shot, I smile at people I meet, I have money to spend.'

46 Write rules for other oft-used words. Such as Failure, Accomplishment, Happiness, Wealth, Sadness, Guilt, Winning, and Losing.

☑ Taking Action

Throughout this section we are going to talk about taking actions. About how to take the right actions to get the right results that you want in life. In this taking action section we are going to be looking at where we are now, where we want to be, and how to do visualisations and a new way.

47 Help yourself take action with this six stage process:

✓ Where are you now?
✓ How did you get here?
✓ Where are you going?
✓ Why do you want to go there?
✓ What are the possible obstacles?
✓ What are you going to do?

48 Repeat this for different situations. Friends, Financial Matters, Career, Learning, Relationship, Emotions, Accomplishments, Social, Physical, Self-esteem, Health.

49 Visualise. Many people struggle with visualisation and I have, in the past. I always thought that everyone was seeing a full 'Cinemascope' film running in their minds. I now know that you can intensely *feel* the pictures, or see and hear the words. Each person has their own way of visualising, and it is only the 'visual' word that makes people think it must be pictures.

50 Improve your visualisation. Look at a scene, any scene, for a second or two and then close your eyes. Now conjure up that scene in your mind. Alternatively, sit in a comfortable chair, with your head upright and your back straight – erect but not stiff. Close your eyes. Lift your head to 20 to 25 degrees above the horizontal. Imagine that you are looking at a television screen about ten feet away from you.

51 Stand up or sit up. Changing your physiology in this way will make you feel more positive.

52 Have a positive outlook. Doesn't it feel great when nothing can stop you from accomplishing anything you want? Make a note of how you feel, look and talk when positive.

53 Go to the other end of the scale. Say negative things like, 'I'm no good, I can't do it, I'm too old. Make a note of your posture, the way you talk, look, and feel. Which end of the scale are you going to live your life?

54 Fake it 'til you make it. You cannot save up your energy so lets start using it. When you meet someone and they ask 'How are you?', what do you say? I have found that over 90% of the world say 'Fine'. I think 'Fine' could well stand for Feeling Inwardly Negative Everyday. You could say 'tremendous' 'great' or 'fantastic'.

55 Retune your strings. By this I mean, it will take some effort to find a new word other than 'fine' that you are comfortable with. It will then take time to get used to using it.

56 Anticipate great things. We all take actions in direct relationship to the pictures, the feelings and the words we use to describe ourselves. If we anticipate getting the results we require, then we will be confident and feel positive.

57 Examine the reasons why people don't take action. Check that none of these reasons hold you back:

- ✓ Lack of motivation
- ✓ Held back by chains
- ✓ Fear
- ✓ Living by the rules imposed by others
- ✓ No definition of success
- ✓ No knowledge of what actions to take
- ✓ Poor dealings with other people
- ✓ Poor time management
- ✓ Lack of understanding about the brain
- ✓ No use of creative skills
- ✓ Stress through lack of planning
- ✓ No financial planning
- ✓ Poor use of communication skills
- ✓ No persistency and no consistency
- ✓ Perfectionism
- ✓ No decision made to take action.

58 Make decisions. Live your life through decisions rather than habits. You will have more control over your life, and enjoy greater success.

59 Ask 'opposing questions' as well as 'confirming questions'. Ask questions that prove that something cannot be done, as well as the more normal questions that prove something can be done. This makes the right decision more apparent.

60 Plan. Making decisions, or lack of making decisions can come down to lack of planning. I think of planning as a four step process, as this diagram shows:

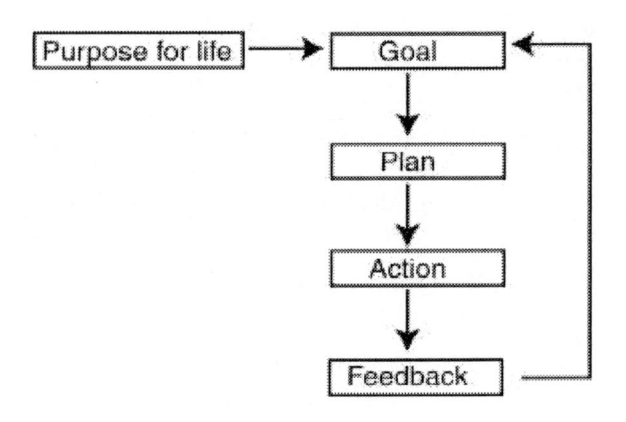

```
Purpose for life ──▶ Goal ◀──┐
                      │      │
                      ▼      │
                     Plan    │
                      │      │
                      ▼      │
                    Action   │
                      │      │
                      ▼      │
                   Feedback ─┘
```

It's a very simple process:

61 Set goals. The goals indicate the plan.

62 Set the plan. This indicates the actions you need to take.

63 Take action.

64 Get feedback. The feedback allows you to adjust the goals, and go back through the system.

65 Use the Maradonna Principle. Diego Maradonna was considered, at one time, to be the best player in the world. What usually happened to him was that he when he had possession of the ball he would be tripped up. Why? Simply because he was trying to score. The only time you get tripped up in life is when you are trying to score! If we have decided to play, we must also accept that with that territory come the knocks, the fouls, the trip-ups.

66 Get up again. I said earlier there are no failures, just lessons to be learned. I have learned some hard lessons. Getting up and taking enthusiastic action is the key.

Conditioning

You've heard of Russian Scientist Ivan Pavlov, the Noble Prize winner who experimented with dogs. Pavlov gave his dogs food and at the same time rang a bell. The dogs became conditioned and salivated when they heard a bell ringing. They developed a conditioned response to a conditioned stimulus. How can we use this knowledge?

67 Create a negative habit circuit breaker. When you find yourself saying or thinking something negative, have a penalty. This will erase negativity.

68 Use the switch method. Feel the feeling you want. Remember that you are already used to saying positive things, acting positively, getting into that state of mind and body. Now you are feeling really positive, create a switch. It could be a clenched fist, a pinch on the arm, a spot on the back of your neck, standing on one leg, it can be anything you choose. Get into the state again and again and again. Keep pressing the switch. Now whenever you press that switch you will feel those positive feelings again.

✓ Dealing with Others

This section is all about dealing with other people. Why people like you and respect you, more about self-management and making the changes to improve your relationships with others. Learning from other people and how we are influenced by those around us and some basics of leadership and understanding.

69 Have esteem for people. This is one of the best ways to deal with people. Try to build self-esteem in people by praising their actions. This must not be false or a technique, because you'll be seen through.

70 Compliment the action, not the person. Compliments aimed direct to the person can sound sugary or sycophantic. Whereas compliments aimed at the actions that people have taken are far more acceptable.

71 Support people. Trying to convince someone to go along your road may be a good idea; however, if they are determined to follow their own path, support them. They will respect you for it and return your support.

72 Like people. For people to like you, you have to like them. We like people who like us, in exactly the same way as people like us if we like them. If you can be genuinely interested in other people, they will have a greater interest in you.

73 See yourself, as others see you. This is one of the best ways to improve our dealings with those people. How would your parents describe you? How would your employees describe you? How would your children describe you?

74 Ask yourself these four questions. Imagine you are your friend, or brother or sister, or child…how would they answer these questions about you?

- ✓ What do you like about this person?
- ✓ What do you dislike about this person?
- ✓ What skills, attributes and attitudes would you like to keep in this person?
- ✓ What skills, attributes and attitudes would you change in this person?

75 Write questions out. As already said, we usually have most of the answers to life's questions. We just need to access the information. The easiest way to do this is write questions out, and let your brain supply the answers.

76 Encourage people to be 'can do' people. This is especially important in children. If you tell children 'Don't drop the plate', the brain translates this as 'drop the plate…don't'. By the time they get the 'don't' it is too late. So we say 'Hold onto the plate firmly'.

77 Decide to have happy relationships. One of the killers of marriages and relationships can be jealousy. Jealousy is the effect, no trust is the cause. To have happy relationships, you have to… decide!

78 Involve partners in the decision making process. On a piece of paper, write a question to yourself. For example 'What do I need to do, be or have to have a happy marriage?'. Get your partner to do the same and then swap your papers.

79 Find time to be just yourself. In relationships, it is important that we recognise the psychological need for privacy, for time for the self. So often situations can arise where people are always somebody else's 'something'.

☑ A Secure Base

One of the first principles of any accomplishment is to have a secure base. We cannot jump from sand, we can only jump from bricks. A secure base, particularly a secure relationship base, is essential for all accomplishment.

80 Learn something from everyone you meet. There isn't much that is new in the world, just tried and tested and proven ideas presented in a different way. However, everyone you meet can teach you something new. Listen to ideas of people who are already doing what you want to do, and then just do the same!

81 Examine and test advice. If you take advice on trust then you may be misled and make a mistake. So be prepared to examine, test and sometimes ignore advice. Sometimes you will know best.

82 Mix with the right people. Can you describe the people who can help you achieve your goals? I am sure you can. Are you mixing with them? If not why not?

✅ Leadership and Teamwork

People, I have always found do not want to be managed, they want to be led. Nobody has ever heard of a world manager – a world leader perhaps.

83 Manage tasks, lead people. If you are in a management role, teach your people self-management. This will build a secure base of people to work with.

84 Lead. Leaders are 'can do' people. They are not afraid of taking action. They are enthusiastic and proactive.

85 Be confident. Leaders have confidence in the people they lead, in their ideas and in themselves.

86 Have vision. In Martin Luther King's unforgettable words: 'I have a dream'.

87 Create a slogan. For example: TEAM – Together Everyone Achieves More? A slogan confirms that you are a 'can do' team.

✅ Interaction

Well, how are we going to improve our interaction, our dealings with others?

88 Actively listen. Do not listen passively. We must use our ears and mouth in relationship to the number we have of each – two ears and one mouth.

89 Ask questions. This is the best way to make sure you understand what is being said.

90 Avoid finishing other people's sentences. Pause before you reply too. This indicates that you are thinking about what was being said.

91 Open conversations the right way. In response to the question 'how are you?'…reply 'tremendous!'

92 Prepare openings. Have questions or statements ready that will start conversations.

93 Deal with prevarication swiftly. You can use the Benjamin Franklin Idea for this. Draw a line down the centre of a piece of paper. Write plus above one column and minus above the other. List all the points for and against and then cross off those that balance each other out. The answers left provide the solution.

94 Close the sale. This is one of the main qualities everyone should learn. Ask 'Should we go ahead then?'

95 Be proactive. In all our dealings with other people, we need to be proactive. If we are waiting for others to take the lead, we might have to wait a long time.

96 Criticise with care. There are times in our dealings with people when we feel that we really do have to criticise an action that has been taken. The important word here is 'action'. It is too hard to criticise the person.

☑ Time Management

What benefits will you receive? Well, you'll get more done, you'll be more in control of your life and time, you'll have numerous ideas to squeeze more out of each and every day. Scientific tests have shown that when man is deprived of all time-measuring devices, after a few days of disorientation, he will return to a functioning cycle of approximately 24 hours in length. Having looked at a number of books, tapes, and seminars, I have come to a startling conclusion:

There is no such thing as time management!

Time is simply a perception. A convenient way in which we measure the passage of hours, days, months, seasons and years. Getting more done is really about self-management, so we do more in the time. My suggestions therefore are:

97 Set your alarm an hour earlier. I know if you are a late riser, you are saying: 'Peter you're crazy!'. Yet I still ask you to try it. You will find that after a few days, you have reduced your sleep need by an hour.

98 Focus. Perhaps some of the reasons people have a problem with time include: Negative self-image, Low self-esteem, Self-doubt, Fear of failure, Fear of making the wrong decision, Rationalisations, Distractions, Lack of urgency, No specific goals, Too busy with low priority tasks, Procrastination, Poor self-management. Deal with these and you will be able to focus.

99 Work smart. Only work on things that will bring the results you want.

100 Deal with interruptions. Have a screening process for telephone calls. Let people know when you do not want to be disturbed.

101 Delegate. If someone can do the same task you are doing less expensively and just as well, then delegate. If someone can do something faster, perhaps they have more authority than you, delegate to them! With all delegation make sure there is a time frame, and that you pass on the authority with the task to get the job done.

102 Say no. If you've found yourself saying yes when you wish you'd said no, try this idea. Write no on every evening in your diary for the rest of the year. This is not to say that you will always say no. It will just remind you that you can say no.

103 Keep a 1-31 file. The 1-31 represent each day in the month. In each file you place a document or note to remind you to write to or call someone or take some action on that day.

104 Create systems. For example: If you have people you write to regularly, saying the same thing, agree to just send this sort of letter:

Dear Stuart
Usual letter.
Sincerely,
Peter.

You can do similar things for telephone calls and meetings…

☑ Mind and Brain

In this section we are going to look at two fascinating areas. We examine how a better understanding of the mind and brain will help you in your aim for more accomplishment. We'll start with memory, how it works, explain an excellent way of dealing with the multiplitude of information that comes your way, give keys to memory and describe a system that you will be able to use to increase your memory.

105 Use memory hooks. To start with create a main list which can be used as a hook for all procedures.

1 Tea, 2 Noah, 3 May, 4 Ray, 5 Law, 6 Jaw, 7 Key, 8 Fee, 9 Pea, 0 The sound is Sh or Zz.

Go through the list and lock the words and numbers into your mind.

Tea . Remember this by thinking about a capital T only having one down stroke, just like number 1.

Noah. Noah has a capital N which has two down strokes, and so is number 2.

May. A capital M has three straight lines, so that's 3.

Ray. Imagine a ray of light coming out of a torch. The torch light is in the shape of a 4.

Law. Imagine a policeman putting his hand up, with four fingers and a thumb, so that's 5.

Jaw. If you look at someone in profile, you will see the number 6 in the shape underneath their chin.

Key. Imagine a brass 7 is a key, undoing a lock.

Fee. If you squash an eight it looks like a pound sign. Pound signs are used in fees.

Pea. If we take a capital P and turn it around, we have a 9.

The sound Sh or Zz, you will simply remember as 0.

Now the final thing to do is use your imagination to link each item to another item. Try this list of ten things:

Table, Chair, Television, Mouse, Car, Dog, Golf ball, Briefcase, Plate, Boat.

For example, to remember item 1 you need to link a table to Tea. In your mind think of a picture of a large cup of tea, enormous, let's say two metres wide. Then, again in your mind, pick up the table and throw it into the tea! That creative image will be easy to remember.

106 Use the six keys to memory: UnUsUaL, Linking, Firsts, Lasts, Repetition, Enthusiasm! You can see how we did this above.

☑ Conscious Mind and Subconscious Mind

The conscious mind is the screen of our computer. The subconscious is our database of information. The subconscious doesn't judge information, it just deals with it.

107 Imagine practising a skill. There has been extensive research that shows imagining improving in a skill will have a similar effect to actually practising that skill more.

108 Ask a useful question. Even if you do not answer the question consciously, you do answer. For example, if you ask yourself what colour your eyes are, the answer just pops up.

109 Relax before visualisation. This enables you to access your subconscious. One method is to tense your body and hold it for a count of ten. Then completely let go.

110 Exercise the eyes. You can strengthen the muscle that focuses the eye, and improve visual tension. Focus on something that is a few centimetres away. Without moving your eyes, focus on something in the distance. Do this for no more than a minute at a time, to avoid eye strain. Alternatively, look in the following directions for no more than thirty seconds. Up-right, Up-left, Down-right, Down-left, Side-left, Side-right. These activities can enhance memory and creativity.

111 Start a knowledge gathering plan. We currently only use about 5% of our brain's capacity. Perhaps look into more listening skills, speed reading skills, vocabulary…

112 Relieve minor aches and pains. For example, when you have a headache. Ask yourself: What shape is the pain? What colour is it? What smell does it have? How does it feel? What does it sound like? Keep coming up with crazy answers and the pain will go away.

113 Read a book like a jigsaw. This idea was developed by Tony Buzan to read reports and books more quickly. With a jigsaw you find all the edges. If a piece won't fit, you put it to one side, totally confident that it will eventually fall into place.

114 Daydream. Einstein came up with his theory of relativity whilst sitting on a grassy bank daydreaming of riding a sunbeam. We can daydream to be more creative.

115 Turn a problem on its head. Ask yourself the question that solves the exact opposite problem, and then reverse the answers. Again you will have more creative solutions.

116 Dare to be different. Often people come up with ideas and then don't have sufficient belief in them to give them a try. Let's just do it….

117 Decide to use this information. Become the head of *Me Unlimited* and I know you will accomplish whatever you want!

☑ Summary

For a more full insight into these ideas, please see my book 'The Pinnacle Principle – How to Maximise your Potential' and for more information on communication, 'The Secrets of Communication - Be Heard and Get Results'.

Peter Thomson

Biography.

Peter Thomson is now regarded as the UK's leading strategist on personal and business growth. Starting in business in 1972 he built 3 successful companies – selling the last to a public company, after only 5 years trading, enabling him to retire at age 42.

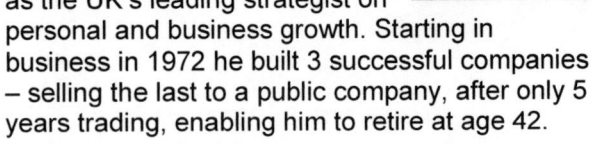

Peter is now Chairman of Peter Thomson International plc and spends his time sharing his proven methods for business and personal success via audio and video programmes, books, seminars and conference speeches.

With over 60 audio programmes written and recorded he is Nightingale Conant's leading UK author.

Peter is the publisher, writer and presenter of the widely acclaimed personal development audio newsletter "The Achievers Edge!" And "The Accelerated Business Growth System"- a monthly CD Video, CD Audio and Action Planner. He is also the author of tgiMondays PLUS - a weekly Motivational Monday Message - Monthly Audio CD - Quarterly Book and Yearly Telephone Seminar.

The American Intercontinental University in London – with permission granted by the American Government - awarded Peter an Honorary Doctorate (Doctor of Letters) for his work in communication skills and helping others to succeed in life.

As a family man (4 sons), 30 years of business experience on his own account and as a keen golfer his presentations and audio works are brought to life with true stories of success and failure - designed and delivered to make any listener realise that they too can achieve their goals, be more successful and live the life they want!

A hallmark of Peter's work is his use of thought-provoking original expressions - expressions that stop people in their mental tracks and have them re–evaluate their beliefs about success.

"People will never consistently do - who they aren't!"

"Better the right "no" answer than the wrong "yes" answer!"

"Most people never ask you the real question - they ask a question about the wrong answer!"

"Ask yourself the *EASY* questions and you'll have a *HARD* life, ask yourself the *HARD* questions and you'll have an *EASY* life!"

"Time and distance travelled compounds the effect of error!"

"If it's too easy you don't care to try - if it's too hard you don't dare to try!"

"In a world where the big things make little difference - it's the LITTLE things that make a BIG difference!"

20 Tips to Promote you and your Business with Booklets!

(It can even be customised for you)

1 Send this booklet to your customers at year's end, thanking them for their business.

2 Use this booklet as a "thank you" for a sales appointment.

3 Mail this booklet to your prospect list to stay in touch with them.

4 Offer this booklet free with any purchase during a specific time, with a certain purchase amount, or when opening a new account.

5 Distribute this booklet to prospects at a trade show.

6 Give this booklet as an incentive for completing a questionnaire or survey.

7 Include this booklet as a "thank you" gift when mailing your invoices.

8 Package this booklet as a value-added bonus with a product you sell.

9 Deliver a copy of this booklet to the hands of the first "X" number of people who enter a draw or come to your store.

10 Provide copies of this booklet to people and organisations who can refer business to you.

11 Give the booklet away at a trade fair or exhibition to attract more potential customers to your stand

12 Give a Tips Booklet as an incentive for completing a Customer Survey Form

13 Include a Tips Booklet as a "Thank You" for the order when sending an invoice or statement

14 Bundle or package a Tips Booklet as a value added bonus for ordering a particular product from your range

15 Send an appropriate Tips Booklet to your staff as a reminder of some of the key principles of success - or as a thank you for a job well done

16 Use packs of Tips Booklets as prizes in a raffle or charity appeal

17 Give a Tips Booklet to the first 50 people who come to your shop or business

18 Use a Tips Booklet as a bonus for sponsorship activation

19 Use a Tips Booklet to launch a new product - including product details in the centre pages of the booklet

20 Use a Tips Booklet as a memorable Change of Address card

Other Booklets in the Series...

"117 Handy Haggling Hints! How to Negotiate Win, Win, Win deals"
by Peter Thomson & Derek Arden

"117 Ways to Grab Your Life by the Throat and Really Make it Happen!"
by Peter Thomson

"117 Ways to get Your Audience To Shout More, More, More Every Time You Stand and Speak!"
by Peter Thomson

"117 Ways to Motivate Your Team Without Breaking the Bank!"
by Sharon Thomson

"How to get 1000's of Leads for Free!"
by Peter Thomson

To order more booklets in the series and/or for details of multiple copy discounts go to

www.pti-worldwide.com

Or email: action@pti-worldwide.com

Or call now on +44 (0) 1926 339901